IMAGES
of America

Coney Island's Wonder Wheel Park

The Wonder Wheel is pictured at closing time. (Photograph by Charles Denson.)

On the Cover: The Wonder Wheel is viewed from the Bowery and West Twelfth Street during the 1940s. (Courtesy of Coney Island History Project.)

IMAGES
of America

Coney Island's Wonder Wheel Park

Charles Denson

ISBN 978-1-4671-0483-8

Published by Arcadia Publishing
Charleston, South Carolina

Printed in the United States of America

Library of Congress Control Number: 2019954260

For all general information, please contact Arcadia Publishing:
Telephone 843-853-2070
Fax 843-853-0044
E-mail sales@arcadiapublishing.com
For customer service and orders:
Toll-Free 1-888-313-2665

Visit us on the Internet at www.arcadiapublishing.com

Coney Island's Surf Avenue in the 1880s had the look of a mining town. The Elephant Hotel is at center, and the Sea Beach Palace is at right. Gravesend Bay and the marshes of Coney Island Creek can be seen in the background. (Courtesy of Charles Denson Archive.)

Contents

ACKNOWLEDGMENTS

This project would not have been possible without assistance from the Wonder Wheel families who contributed photographs and historical information for the 2020 exhibit celebrating the 100th anniversary of the Wonder Wheel. Thank you to the Vourderis family of Deno's Wonder Wheel Park, Freddi Hermann, Walter Kerner, Michael Way, Helen Way, Richard Garms, the Ward family, and Patricia Casola. Additional photographs were provided by Abe Feinstein, Jim McDonnell, Dan Pisark, and Tricia Vita.

And a very special thank-you to Stacy Vourderis and Carol Hill Albert, whose love of history and preservation makes it all possible.

Please visit the Coney Island History Project for more information at www.coneyislandhistory.org.

Introduction

The story of the Wonder Wheel is the story of immigration in America. The century-old landmark comes with a narrative: this incredibly complex machine was designed, built, owned, operated, and ultimately saved by immigrants with little formal education who came to the United States penniless and wound up realizing the American Dream. The Wheel's designer, Charles Hermann, was Romanian. Herman Garms, the Wheel's builder and first owner, was German. The Italian, Irish, and Russian immigrant construction workers who built the Wheel became shareholders and part owners. And Greek immigrant Denos Vourderis purchased the Wheel in 1983 and restored it, and his family now owns and operates the amusement park that surrounds it.

Coney Island is not, and never was, an amusement park in the traditional sense. It was a neighborhood composed of small businesses. Rides and attractions were located on city streets and privately owned. There was no fence or closing time. Coney Island was a place where people of small means could start a business and work their way up. Several big parks were located at Coney Island, but mostly the amusement area consisted of independent operators. Each establishment represented the personality or quirks of the owner and operator. Family businesses like Deno's Wonder Wheel Park are what led to Coney Island's success and longevity.

Much of the information in this book is derived from interviews with family members linked to the creation and operation of the Wheel. The Vourderis family, owners and operators of the Wonder Wheel, represent the essence of Coney Island. They're hard workers who treat their employees like family. They also have a profound sense of history and their place in "The World's Playground." Thanks to the Vourderis family, the Wonder Wheel has survived longer than any other amusement in Coney Island. The Wheel is more than an amusement ride. It's a work of art and the ultimate survivor in an ephemeral world—a link to Coney's remarkable past.

A young Charles Hermann is pictured after he arrived in New York in 1907. (Courtesy of Freddi Hermann.)

One

Charles Hermann

Charles Hermann, the inventor of the Wonder Wheel, didn't care about money. "He had no business sense and would leave a 20¢ tip for a 5¢ cup of coffee," his daughter Helen remembers. "All he cared about was creating." It's unfortunate and ironic that the man who designed and built Coney Island's greatest ride never realized a penny of profit from it.

Hermann was an inventor of unusual things. Among his early patents and inventions were a cowcatcher for automobiles, designed to prevent injury to pedestrians; a radio coupler for freight trains; a directional traffic light; push-button radio tuners; and the GyroGlobe. He never profited from any of them. Hermann's lasting legacy is his invention of a "perpetual motion machine" that became a spectacular Coney Island amusement device called the Wonder Wheel.

Born in the Transylvanian Alps of Romania in 1890, Hermann grew up in Bucharest and was trained as a machinist. After immigrating to the United States in 1907, he found work at the Brooklyn Navy Yard and the Happel Iron Works in Manhattan. In 1912, he moved out west for a job at the Union Iron Works in San Francisco. It was in San Francisco that Hermann began dreaming about creating amusements.

The sprawling Panama-Pacific International Exposition opened in San Francisco in 1915. It was a marvelous 636-acre venue that celebrated the opening of the Panama Canal and also showed the world that the city had recovered from the devastation of the 1906 earthquake. The exposition had an extensive amusement zone that included a spectacular device made of steel trusses called the Aeroscope. Hermann, who loved working with steel, was hooked. The Aeroscope was designed by Joseph Strauss, the engineer who would later design the Golden Gate Bridge; it may have inspired Hermann's 1914 design of his first perpetual motion machine.

Hermann and three friends obtained an unusual advertising job. They teamed up with a donkey-drawn wagon and walked across the country from San Francisco to New York extolling the wonders of the exposition. They were dubbed "4 Jackasses and a Donkey." Mayor James Rolph of San Francisco provided them a letter of introduction to New York mayor John Mitchel. The letter stated that "the purpose of their expedition is to see the country, and, incidentally, to bear the message of our Exposition across the continent." They started out on April 8, 1915.

This was also the year that Hermann received approval of a patent for what would one day become the Wonder Wheel. This early version of an eccentric Ferris wheel was filed in August 1914 for a ride with open upholstered cars that rolled off the wheel onto a platform where the riders entered and exited before rolling to the other side and reattaching to the wheel. The design had a strong resemblance to Leonardo da Vinci's sketches for a perpetual motion machine.

Upon reaching New York, Hermann found work as custodian and manager of the Rochambeau Apartments on St. Nicholas Avenue and 182nd Street in Manhattan. One of the tenants in the building was a German immigrant named Herman Garms. Garms had the innate business sense that Hermann lacked and showed interest in the device that Hermann had patented. The two formed a corporation called the Eccentric Ferris Wheel Company and set about procuring a location in the heart of the amusement universe, a place called Coney Island.

Hermann was the dreamer, and Garms was the realist. When Hermann informed Garms that he had plans for a perpetual motion machine, Garms said, "No you don't! Make it a wheel, keep the cars on it, and we'll make it an amusement ride." Hermann redesigned the ride into what he called Dip the Dip, and they set out for Coney Island.

William J. Ward, the wealthy patriarch of a pioneering Coney Island family, found just the right spot for them, a vacant parcel on Jones Walk that had recently been cleared of a deadly roller coaster called Roosevelt's Rough Riders. Ward was so impressed with Hermann's big wheel proposal that he became an investor and offered his land in exchange for a share of future profits, a partnership that lasted until his death in 1936.

As World War I came to a close in 1918, construction of the wheel got off to a shaky start. Garms began raising funds to cover construction by selling shares of stock to family and friends. Hermann insisted on using only expensive Bethlehem Steel, and the partners ran out of money three times during construction. Hermann also insisted on fabricating all the structural steel components onsite and invented a variety of specialized tools to do the work—tools that he failed to patent, unfortuntately. There were other setbacks, including design changes to the wheel's massive concrete foundation and postwar shortages of materials.

The Great Steel Strike of 1919 also threatened the project. Garms had hired a team of faithful immigrant workers. "They were all Russian Jews, Italians, and Irish," Garms's grandson Rick Garms said, "and he treated them well." When union officials showed up at the worksite, they complained that the workers weren't union members and wanted to shut down the project. Garms responded by making the workers shareholders in the company and giving them stock. "They're not workers," he said. "They're owners!" This arrangement had never been attempted before, and the wheel project unofficially became a cooperative.

Completed in 1920, the Wonder Wheel was a magnificent machine. With swinging and stationary cars, it was a combination of roller coaster, Ferris wheel, and observation tower. It heralded the new Coney Island of the Roaring Twenties. True to character, Charles Hermann, inventor of the wheel and a man with no business sense, had sold every share of his stock to complete the project and lost all ownership in the process.

Hermann walked away from the Wonder Wheel and left it in the hands of Herman Garms, whose family would operate it for the next 60 years. He moved to the Bronx, where he found a job as a building superintendent and began designing his next project in a basement workshop. He soon had a scale model of a wheel he called the Giant Coaster Wheel, a 325-foot structure that would be the biggest in the world, bigger than Ferris's wheel for Chicago's 1893 World's Fair. He later offered it to planners of the 1939–1940 New York City World's Fair, but they rejected it because it would have been larger than the Trylon and Perisphere, the symbols of the fair.

His last invention was the GyroGlobe, an enormous steel orb that resembled a gyroscope. The overengineered contraption, built of heavy riveted steel, operated at Coney Island across the street from the Wheel for many years before being moved to Long Beach, California. It was not a financial success.

In the years after the Wonder Wheel opened, Charles Hermann rarely visited Coney Island. Sometimes he would take his family by subway from the Bronx for a ride on the Wheel, but it was usually his wife's idea. Hermann's daughter Helen remembers her father as a loner. "He was happiest when working with his hands. He was an individualistic guy and did things his own way. He didn't care about fashion or what anyone else thought about him. He didn't care about money or fame. Once the Wheel was up and running, he moved on."

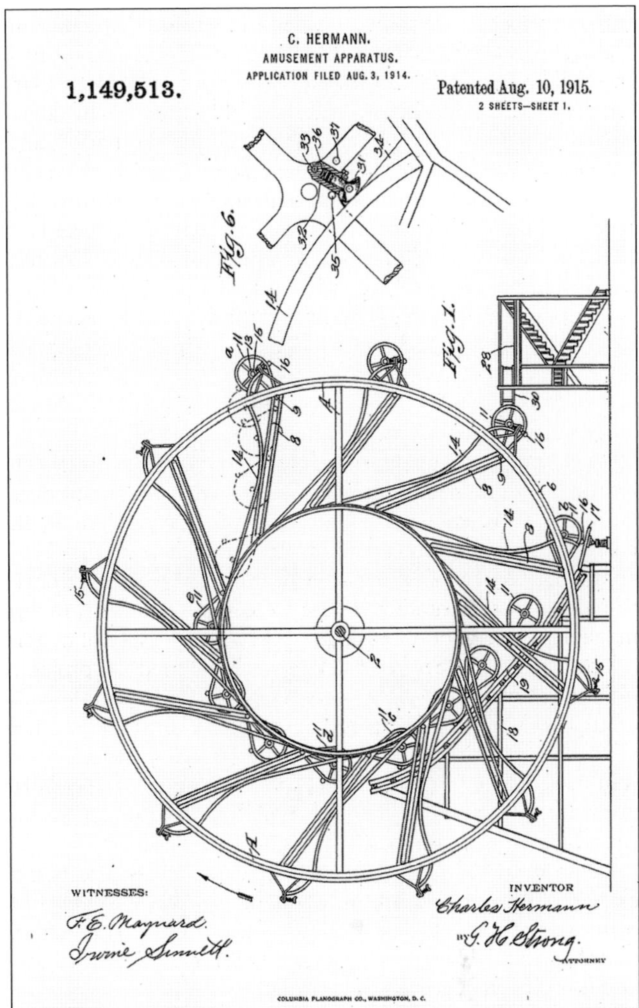

Charles Hermann's patent for his eccentric amusement wheel, filed in San Francisco in 1914, bears a remarkable resemblance to Leonardo da Vinci's 15th-century sketches for a perpetual motion machine. (Courtesy of Coney Island History Project.)

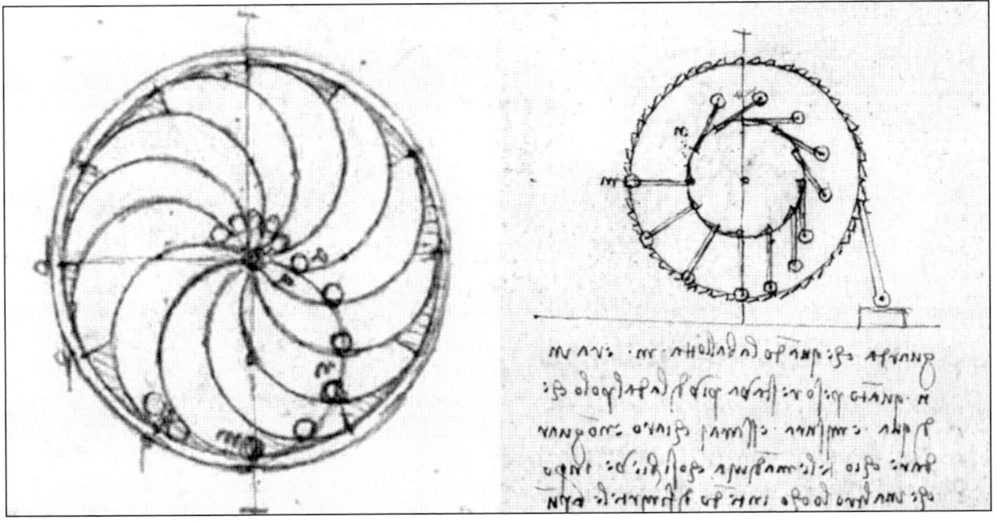

Leonardo da Vinci sketched his machine in the Codex Forster notebook around 1495. (Courtesy of Victoria and Albert Museum.)

In April 1915, Charles Hermann and three friends left San Francisco and walked to New York with a donkey cart to advertise the Panama-Pacific International Exposition. They were dubbed "4 Jackasses and a Donkey." Three of the four are seen above. (Courtesy of Hermann family.)

The 1915 exposition sparked Hermann's desire to build a giant steel amusement device that eventually became the Wonder Wheel. Construction of the 636-acre fair began in 1914. It opened in February 1915 and closed in December the same year. (Courtesy of Coney Island History Project.)

Joseph Strauss's Aeroscope at the Panama-Pacific Exposition demonstrated the possibilities of dynamic steel amusement devices. The steel arm carried an observation deck that held 120 passengers. For 25¢, one could rise 235 feet into the air and get a sweeping view of San Francisco. Two decades later, Strauss designed the Golden Gate Bridge. (Courtesy of Charles Denson Archive.)

George Washington Ferris constructed his 264-foot wheel for the 1893 Chicago World's Fair. Charles Hermann was determined build a bigger one. The Ferris Wheel operated at two other locations before being permanently dismantled. (Courtesy of Coney Island History Project.)

COPY OF OFFICIAL NOTICE OF FINAL ALLOWANCE

DEPARTMENT OF THE INTERIOR
UNITED STATES PATENT OFFICE
WASHINGTON, D.C.

Mr. Charles Hermann, January 7, 1915.
Care of DEWEY, STRONG & CO.
San Francisco Cal.

Sir: Your Application for a patent for an Improvement in AMUSEMENT APPARATUS, Filed August 3, 1914, Serial Number 854,696 has been examined and allowed.

The final fee, TWENTY DOLLARS, must be paid not later than SIX MONTHS from the date of this present notice of allowance.

If the final fee is not paid within that period the patent will be with-held, and your only relief will be a renewal of the application, with additional fees, under the provisions of Section 4897, Revised Statutes. The office delivers patents upon the day of their date, and on which their term begins to run. The printing, photo-lithographing and engrossing of the several patent parts, preparatory to final signing and sealing, will require about four weeks, and such work will not be undertaken until after payment of the necessary fees.

If you desire to have the patent issue to ASSIGNEES, an assignment containing a REQUEST to that effect, together with the FEE for recording the same must be filed in this office on or before the date of payment of final fee.

Final fees will not be received from other than the applicant, his assignee or attorney, or a party in interest as shown by the records of the Patent Office.

Respectfully,
E. B. MOORE,
Commissioner of Patents.

Twenty-four-year-old Charles Hermann designed his first "amusement apparatus" while making a living as a steelworker in San Francisco. His patent was first filed on August 3, 1914, and was accepted in 1915. (Courtesy of Hermann family.)

MAYOR'S OFFICE
San Francisco

April 5, 1915.

Hon. John Purroy Mitchel,
Mayor's Office,
New York City, N.Y.

Dear Mr. Mayor:

Three young men, Charles Hermann, Sydney Walkerdine and Chas.W.Green, residents of this city, plan to start on a walking tour to New York City, leaving here Thursday, April 8th. The purpose of their expedition is to see the country, and, incidentally, to bear the message of our Exposition across the continent.

All three bear excellent reputations and have my good wishes for a pleasant and successful journey. I Commend them to a kind reception at your hands, and take this means of extending to you a most cordial invitation to visit San Francisco [illegible] Exposition period.

With best personal regards, I am,

Yours sincerely,

[signature]
Mayor.

This letter from the mayor of San Francisco to the mayor of New York introduces Hermann and explains his 1915 donkey-cart expedition across the continent. (Courtesy of Hermann family.)

Charles Hermann built this scale model of the Giant Coaster Wheel, designed for the 1939–1940 New York City World's Fair. He built the model in the basement of a Bronx apartment house where he worked as a custodian. (Courtesy of Michael Way.)

Uncle Sam's Cannon Ride, on West Twelfth Street, was one of the dozens of novelty coasters built during the Victorian era. These amusements usually had a short life. (Courtesy of Charles Denson Archive.)

A World War I bond drive is held in front of William J. Ward's Bank of Coney Island, located on Surf Avenue and West Twelfth Street. Ward provided a site for the Wonder Wheel. (Courtesy of Charles Denson Archive.)

George C. Tilyou, like Hermann, was influenced by Ferris's Chicago wheel and had a smaller one built at Coney Island. He billed it as the largest in the world, but it wasn't. The device opened on Surf Avenue and West Fifth Street and was later moved to his Steeplechase Park in 1897. (Courtesy of Charles Denson Archive.)

Tilyou's wheel stood side-by-side with Thompson and Dundy's Giant See-Saw at Steeplechase Park, where Hermann could see the possibilities of these dynamic steel amusements. (Courtesy of Charles Denson Archive.)

William J. Ward, a prominent businessman, was instrumental in the development of Coney Island beginning in the 1870s. He owned a bank, hotels, bathhouses, restaurants, and a vast tract of beachfront property. He also founded the Coney Island Chamber of Commerce and built Coney Island's first boardwalk. Ward became a partner in the Eccentric Ferris Wheel Amusement Company, founded by Hermann and Garms, and provided the Jones Walk site for the Wheel. (Courtesy of Coney Island History Project.)

Ward's boardwalk is pictured at the beginning of the 20th century. The brick building at right is the entrance to Ward's bathhouse. These quaint and flimsy beachfront businesses would be demolished soon after the construction of the new boardwalk in 1923. (Courtesy of Charles Denson Archive.)

Bathers are pictured on the beach in front of Ward's bathhouse. (Courtesy of Charles Denson Archive.)

In this crowded beach scene in front of Ward's, the sign at right points the way to the Roosevelt's Rough Riders roller coaster on Jones Walk. A few years, later the coaster would be demolished and replaced with the Wonder Wheel. (Courtesy of Charles Denson Archive.)

Roosevelt's Rough Riders opened in 1907, during Theodore Roosevelt's second term as president. The Bowery entrance to the coaster was ornate, constructed in an elaborate style with flagged towers and archways. The ride had an electric third rail and attendants who dressed in uniforms of soldiers who served with Roosevelt in the Spanish-American War. The scenic railway portion of the ride had an exhibit showing scenes of the war. In the summer of 1915, a horrific accident led to the deaths of three passengers who were thrown from one of the ride's speeding cars to the sidewalk below. Four other passengers were seriously injured, and several had to be rescued while clinging to a handrail high above the street. The ride closed soon after. (Courtesy of Coney Island History Project.)

The Roosevelt's Rough Riders roller coaster was located on the future site of the Wonder Wheel. The domed entrance to the coaster was preserved to house concessions before being demolished for construction of the Wonder Wheel. The ticket below displays a caricature of a delighted Pres. Theodore Roosevelt. (Both, courtesy of Coney Island History Project.)

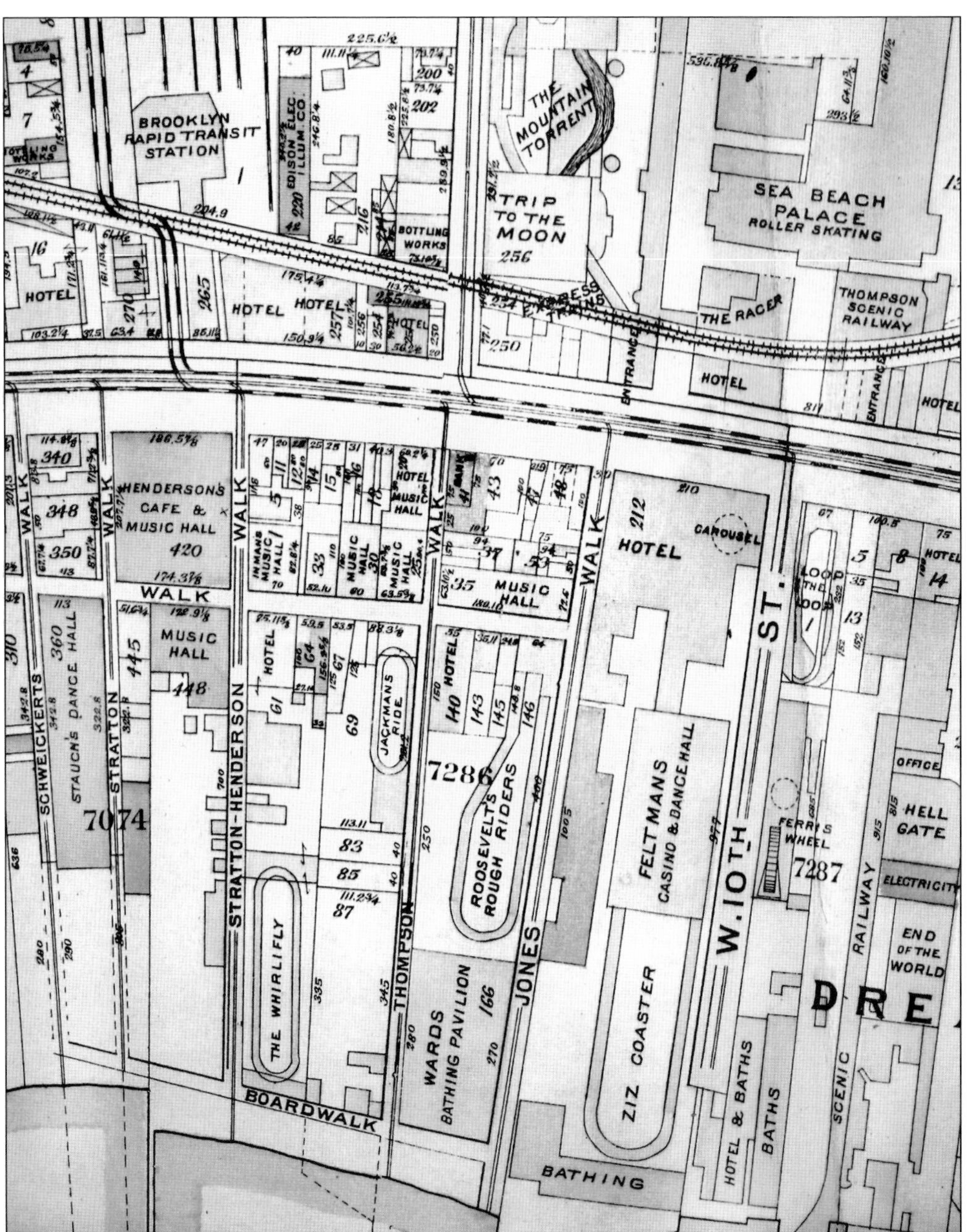

Ward's Bathing Pavilion is at the bottom center of this c. 1907 map, just below the Roosevelt's Rough Riders coaster. William J. Ward owned all of the property between Surf Avenue and the Atlantic Ocean from Jones Walk to Thompson Walk (which was later widened to become West Twelfth Street). The Wonder Wheel would be built on the site where the coaster curves just above Ward's Bathing Pavilion. (Courtesy of Charles Denson Archive.)

This c. 1918 view looks south from a point above Coney Island Creek. Luna Park is in the foreground, and the Atlantic Ocean is above. At the top center is a small Ferris wheel, and Ward's bathhouse is just to the left. The old Rough Riders site has been cleared, and the Wonder Wheel would soon rise just behind the bathhouse. The entrance to the Rough Riders coaster on the Bowery, topped by a dome and two towers, is still standing and would become a concession stand. Other landmarks are the Luna Park tower in the foreground and the Sea Beach Palace at left. (Courtesy of Charles Denson Archive.)

Coney Island was transformed in the 1920s, with brick and steel replacing the ramshackle wood-frame structures along Surf Avenue. The 2,500-seat Loews Theater on Surf Avenue included an office tower above. The building was declared a landmark in 2010 and is now being renovated as a hotel and spa. (Courtesy of Charles Denson Archive.)

The Riegelmann Boardwalk, seen here under construction in July 1922, was built in the ocean, and sand was pumped in from offshore to create a new beach. The city had to buy back the shorefront, as it had been sold off to private individuals in the 1870s. The Wonder Wheel can be seen behind the derrick. (Courtesy of Coney Island History Project.)

William J. Ward was the head of a conglomerate that pooled its resources to build a world-class hotel on the boardwalk. The Half Moon Hotel, named for Henry Hudson's ship, opened in 1927 at the west end of Coney Island. It was the scene of a famous murder mystery when gangster Abe Reles of Murder, Inc., went out a window while being held in protective custody. The building was demolished in 1994. (Courtesy of Charles Denson Archive.)

DIP THE DIP

© 1920 by Science & Invent

Next Summer, Visitors to New York's Playground, Coney Island, Will Be Amused by This Giant 150-Foot "Dip-the-Dip" Whe
Which Combines All the Thrills of the Scenic Railway, the Ferris Wheel and the Chute-the-Chutes.

Coney's New Topsy-Turvy Wheel

An article in a 1920 issue of *Science and Invention* showed the "Topsy-Turvy" wheel sporting a lighted star motif and its original name, Dip the Dip. (Courtesy of Coney Island History Project.)

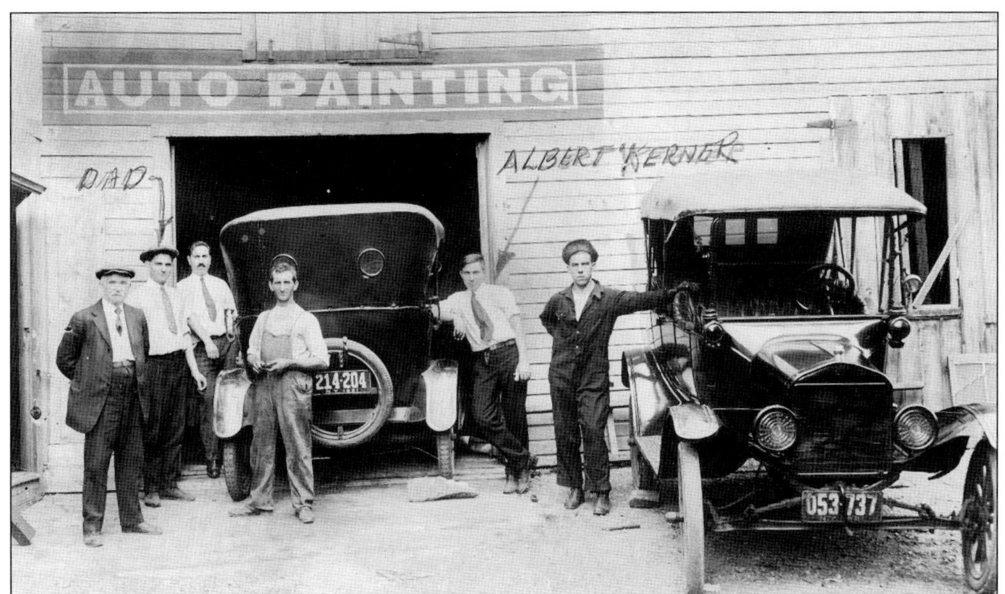

Charles Hermann (labeled "Dad") and Albert Kerner are pictured in Coney Island in 1921. The Kerner and Garms families owned and operated the Wonder Wheel for six decades. (Courtesy of Freddi Hermann.)

NUMBER 20

SHARES 10

INCORPORATED UNDER THE LAWS OF THE STATE OF NEW YORK

THRILLO AMUSEMENT CO., INC.

Capital Stock $50,000 · Par Value $10

This Certifies that Charles Hermann is the owner of TEN Shares of the Capital Stock of THRILLO AMUSEMENT CO., INC. Full Paid and Non-Assessable transferable on the books of this Corporation in person or by Attorney upon surrender of this Certificate properly endorsed.

In Witness Whereof, the said Corporation has caused this Certificate to be signed by its duly authorized officers and its Corporate Seal to be hereunto affixed this 9TH day of August A.D. 1930

Secretary-Treasurer · President

Charles Hermann never made a profit on any of his creations. He only cared about seeing his inventions come to fruition. This 1930 stock certificate gave him 10 shares of the Thrillo Amusement Company. He was also the president of Thrillo. (Courtesy of Freddi Hermann.)

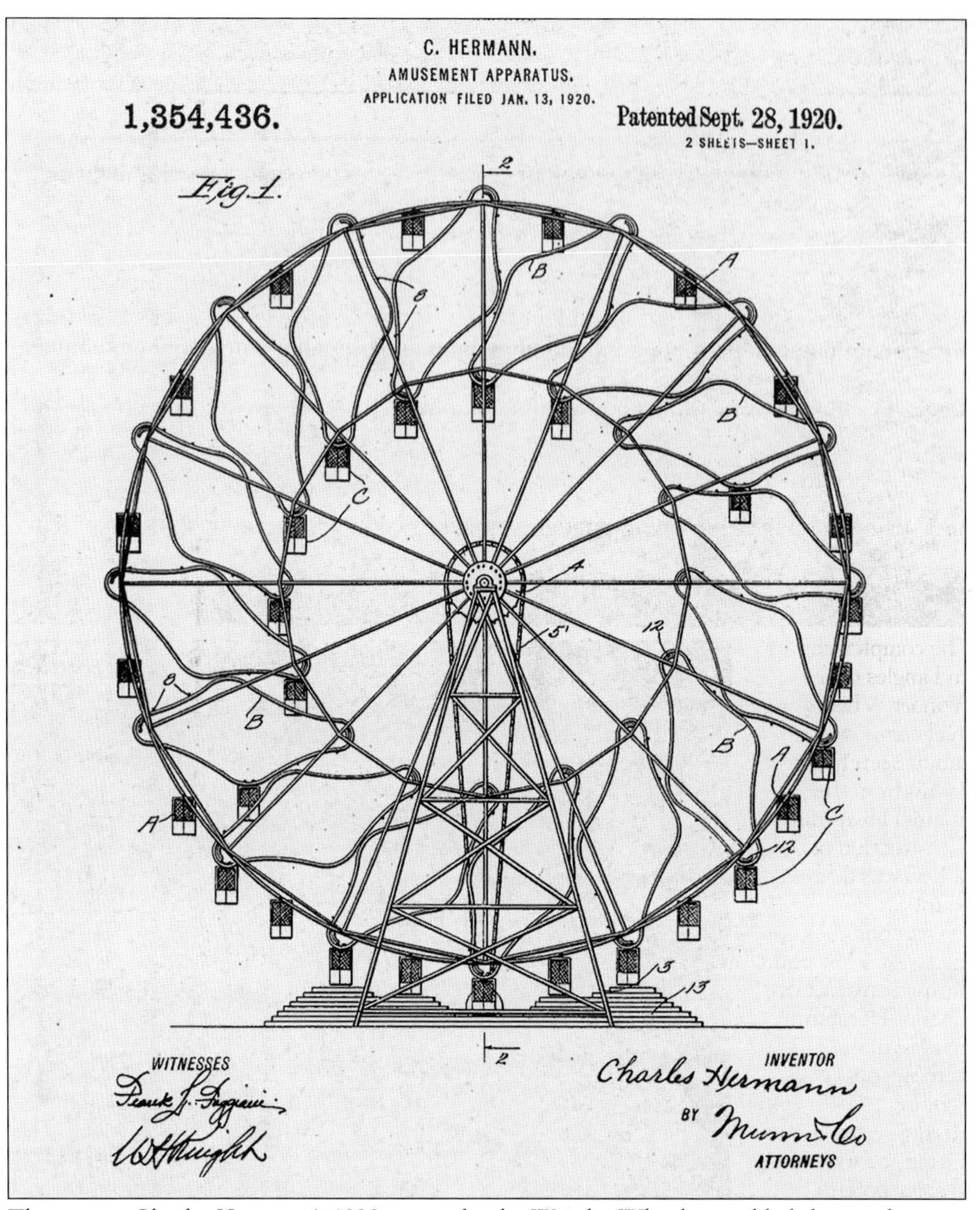

The cars on Charles Hermann's 1920 patent for the Wonder Wheel resembled the weights on a perpetual motion machine. Herman Garms convinced Hermann to give up on perpetual motion and concentrate on amusements. (Courtesy of Coney Island History Project.)

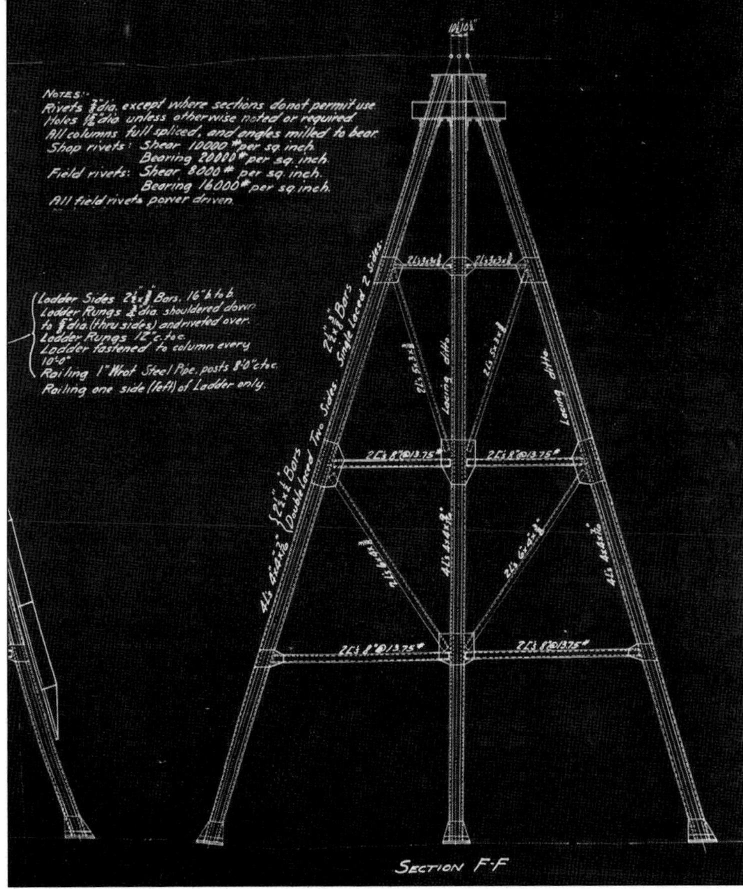

The complex curves and angles of the Wonder Wheel's steel components can be seen in these details from the original blueprints. Construction of the Wheel was delayed countless times as design changes were made. At a low point during construction, Charles Hermann and Herman Garms were the only ones building the Wheel, driving rivets during the winter to show potential shareholders that work was actually going on. (Both, courtesy of Deno's Wonder Wheel.)

The Garms family included (pictured from left to right) Greta, Alfred "Freddie," Herman Jr., and Herman Sr. When Herman married, he changed his name from Herman Rosenfeld to Herman Garms, taking his wife's last name. (Courtesy of Kerner family.)

Two

Herman and Freddy Garms

An accident brought Herman Garms to America. Born in Hamburg, Germany, Garms had nascent careers as a cheesemaker, eel fisherman, and first mate on a pilot tug. The tug turned out to be instrumental in his journey to America. The tug's captain was involved in a drunken accident and made an offer to young Garms: "If you take responsibility for the accident, I'll pay your way to America." Garms took the rap, lost his mate's license, and departed Germany aboard a steamship. After arriving in New York in 1907, he found a new home in Manhattan's Germantown.

Young Herman Garms did what many immigrants do when starting a new life in America: he changed his name and took a new identity. His original name was Herman Rosenfeld. During World War I, he married Gretta Garms and took his wife's last name, preferring the Nordic-sounding Garms to the German Rosenfeld.

Garms did odd jobs around Manhattan and wound up living in an apartment house on the Upper West Side whose custodian was fellow immigrant Charles Hermann. A partnership was formed between Hermann, the idealistic inventor, and Garms, the future businessman. The pair would soon make history at Coney Island by building an amazing structure called the Wonder Wheel.

Herman Garms raised the cash to build Charles Hermann's fantastic invention by forming a corporation with family and local business owners as shareholders. The fledgling partnership survived a series of financial setbacks but accomplished its goal. By the end of 1920, a magnificent steel structure had risen on Jones Walk in the heart of Coney Island.

Coney Island was undergoing a transformation during the 1920s, and the spectacular new Wonder Wheel would serve as the crown jewel of the new beachfront resort. Between 1917 and 1920, the city bought back the beachfront from private owners, and in 1923, it created a new wide beach and boardwalk open to the public. Three new roller coasters, the Thunderbolt, Tornado, and Cyclone, were constructed within a decade, as were two palatial theaters, the RKO Tilyou and the Loew's Coney Island. The 14-story Half Moon Hotel opened on the boardwalk in 1927. William J. Ward was the driving force behind the redevelopment as well as the newly formed Coney Island Chamber of Commerce, founded in 1924. Ward welcomed the Wonder Wheel by providing a home for it.

The Wonder Wheel began as a family-run operation. Garms and his brother-in-law, Alfred Kerner, became partners and operators. Two of Garms's sons, Alfred "Freddie" and Herman Jr., practically grew up working at the Wheel and would run it after Herman's death. The Garms family built a summer home adjacent to the workshop under the Wheel and lived below the ride all season long. A dining room and kitchen under the Wheel became known for ongoing card games and serious after-hours imbibing.

Herman was a man of small stature but a tireless worker. He twice fell from high atop the Wheel, once landing in an apple tree and another time surviving by grabbing a beam with his legs. An accident in the shop crushed his left hand and left his fingers permanently curled and useless, although he could still use his thumb. The doctors wanted to amputate his hand, but his sister-in-law, a nurse, intervened and prevented it. These incidents never slowed him down.

Herman Jr. became the Wheel's main mechanic, and his brother Freddie became the face of the Wheel, albeit a comical face. Unlike his father, Herman, a quiet and humble man, Freddie was a real showman and risktaker, known for stunts that included riding on the rooftops of the swinging cars while in operation and climbing around on the Wonder Wheel untethered. And he loved to drink Chivas Regal scotch.

Freddie served as a tireless Coney Island booster and president of the Coney Island Chamber of Commerce. He enjoyed talking to reporters and spinning wild tales about the Wheel and Coney Island. Every five years, Freddie would throw himself a birthday party, usually at Gargiulo's Restaurant, where he invited scores of guests and gave them all presents. And then came Spook-A-Rama.

The Spook-A-Rama dark ride was installed by Freddie in 1955, at the height of the 1950s horror film craze. Built by the Pretzel Amusement Ride Company, it was billed as the longest spook ride in the world, running up and down Jones Walk for a quarter-mile. A local banner painter and artist named Dan Casola was hired by Freddie to paint signs, and the two wound up creating an incredible variety of animated monster figures and murals, including the much-beloved Cyclops heads that adorned the ride's frontage. Casola wound up working at the Wheel for two decades, creating artwork that has been displayed in museums across the country.

The Wheel's famous neon was also Freddie's concept. He loved neon signs and installed them all over. Rick Garms, Freddie's son, grew up working at the Wheel and recalled his father's obsession. "He put rose-colored neon all over the Wheel's spokes, and we had to take it all down every winter or the ice would destroy the bulbs. We had a crazy Lithuanian guy who designed everything and repaired the tubes and transformers."

The neon displays at the Wheel have been written about as being some of the best examples of neon art in New York, and the classic spinning sign at the Twelfth Street entrance was included in the landmarking in 1989.

Rick also remembers his father putting him to work when he was nine years old. Freddie would let him run the Wheel without riders to attract people or to get the water out of the tracks after rainstorms. Rick was only 13 years old when he obtained his elevator operator license, allowing him to legally operate the ride. "It was hard work," he says. "We had old equipment, we did everything with block and tackle, and we used old railroad jacks to take the cars off." Rick later started his own amusement business but declined to take over the Wheel when his father was considering retirement.

Freddie and his cousin Walter Kerner continued operating the ride, although Coney Island went into a steep decline after the closure of Steeplechase Park in 1964. The ride suffered from benign neglect. Walter and Freddie bought out all the remaining partners in 1970, assuming full ownership until selling to Denos Vourderis in 1983. Not many people were capable of taking over such a daunting machine, but Freddie knew that he had chosen the right buyer, and the Wonder Wheel soon had a new life as the crown jewel of Coney Island.

This early postcard shows the Wheel's new name and the old. The original powerhouse can be seen just below the word "Wheel." It was later moved to ground level. (Courtesy of Charles Denson Archive.)

The Wonder Wheel is pictured during an early phase of construction c. 1920. The Riegelmann Boardwalk had yet to be built, the beach was still private, and access was through the bathhouses that the lined the shore. The Bushman's Baths dance pavilion was built directly on the beach. All of these intrusions were removed when the city took control of the waterfront in 1923. (Courtesy of Dan Pisark.)

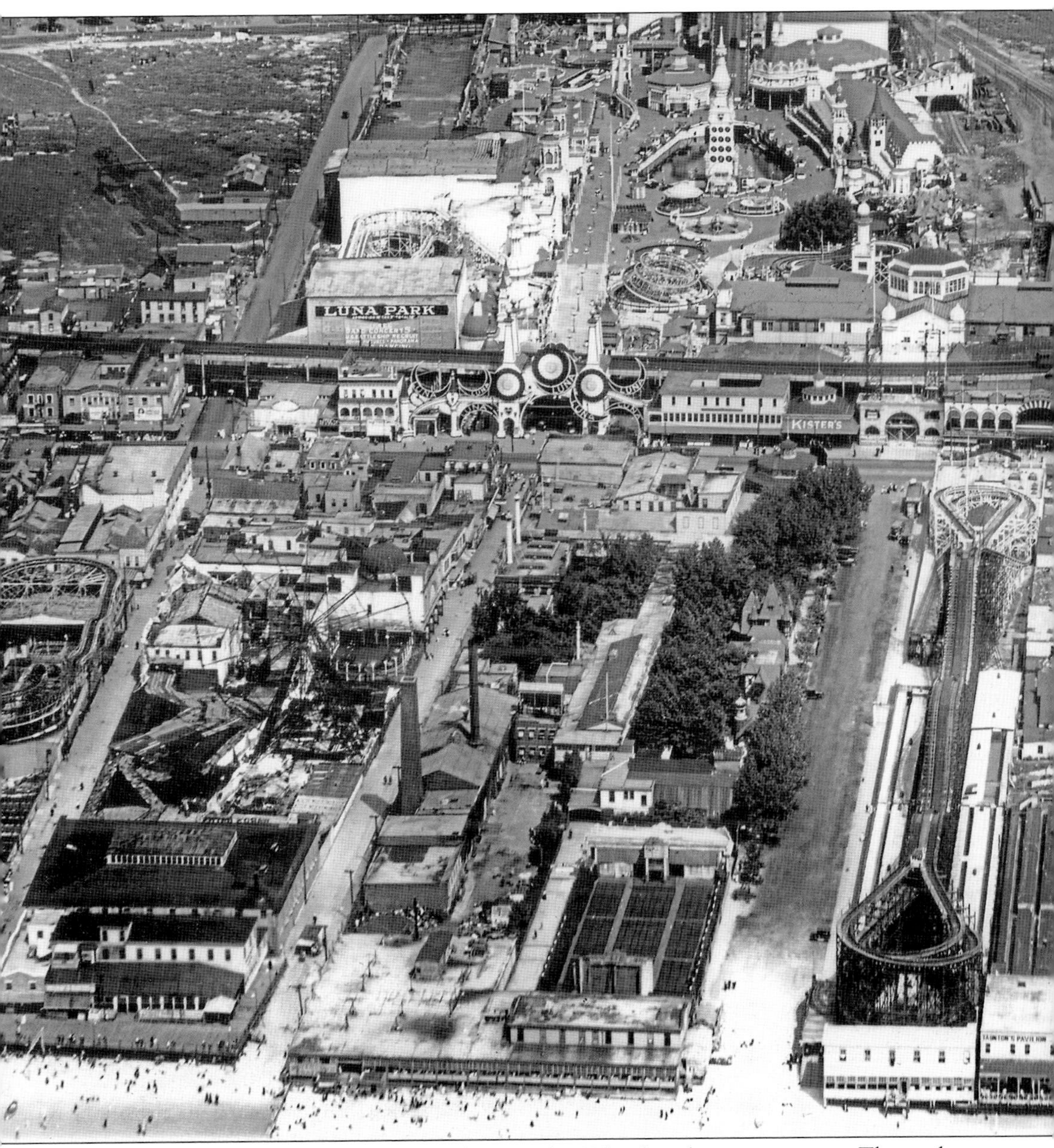

An aerial view shows Coney Island and the Wonder Wheel under construction. The spokes of the partially constructed wheel can be seen to the left of the large chimney of the Feltman powerhouse. Luna Park is at top, and the Giant Racer roller coaster is at right. The coaster to the left of the Wheel is Jackman's Thriller. Feltman's outdoor movie theater is at bottom center. (Courtesy of Charles Denson Archive.)

ECCENTRIC FERRIS WHEEL

This wheel at Coney Island, N. Y., is the only one of its kind in the world. It weighs 150 tons, and has a carrying capacity of 128 persons. It turns, dips and climbs, all in one rotation. It is controlled by the Brown-Hunkele electro-magnetic clutch and brake, and can be stopped almost instantaneously when at full speed.

(Photo from H. E. Cyphers.)

An early story about the Wonder Wheel used an illustration of the Wheel without all of its cars. The Wheel originally ran on DC power but converted to AC current when Coney Island switched to Thomas Edison's power grid in the 1920s. (Courtesy of Charles Denson Archive.)

This 1920s view down Jones Walk from Surf Avenue shows the Wheel without cars in the off-season. The Grashorn Building, at right, survived into the 21st century. Feltman's Restaurant is at left. (Courtesy of Dan Pisark.)

In 1930, a well-dressed family poses on the boardwalk in front of Ward's bathhouse with the Wonder Wheel in the distance. Half of the bathing pavilion, including its beautiful beachfront facade, would be demolished in 1940 when Robert Moses had the boardwalk moved to the north. (Courtesy of Charles Denson Archive.)

WARD'S BATHS

Absolutely Fireproof

Boardwalk and W. 12th St.

CONEY ISLAND

The beautiful new boardwalk entrance to Ward's bathhouse was demolished when the boardwalk was moved in 1941. The fireproof Ward's facility was famous for its "splendid bathing facilities, sun decks, showers, steamrooms." It was "a place to meet your friends and family in a refined atmosphere." (Courtesy of Charles Denson Archive.)

A 1927 view shows the boardwalk in front of Ward's bathhouse. The ornate building was slowly dismantled over the years, and the boardwalk level eventually became Ward's Kiddie Park. A domed Feltman's hot dog kiosk is at right. (Courtesy of Charles Denson Archive.)

This unusual view shows two wheels behind Ocean Baths in the 1920s: the Wonder Wheel at right and a small one at left that had been moved around Coney Island many times. The Wheel had three other Ferris wheel neighbors over the years. (Courtesy of Coney Island History Project.)

The enormous street-level sign advertising Ward's bathhouse on West Twelfth Street in the 1920s was hard to miss. This frontage would host a variety of amusements over the next century. (Courtesy of Charles Denson Archive.)

A snappy-looking crew poses at the Wonder Wheel loading platform during the 1920s. (Courtesy of Charles Denson Archive.)

Young Freddie Garms works one of the games below the Wonder Wheel on Jones Walk. Freddie became quite the showman during the six decades he spent at the Wheel. (Courtesy of Charles Denson Archive.)

Among the many West Twelfth Street amusements was the Looper, a circular steel cage that rolled on a track and was controlled by riders using foot pedals to adjust the speed of the spin. A Looper ride still exists at Knoebels Amusement Resort in Pennsylvania. (Courtesy of Sheila Amato.)

Kiddie's Wonderland, with its giant inflatable horse, set up shop in front of the Wonder Wheel in the 1920s. (Courtesy of Charles Denson Archive.)

The West Twelfth Street location seen above was constantly changing as the Ward family tried new attractions alongside the Wheel during the 1940s. A construction crew unloads lumber to build a new platform behind the Wheel. (Courtesy of Charles Denson Archive.)

During the 1920s, the Bowery entrance to the Virginia Reel served as the Wonder Wheel's front porch. The ride consisted of a circular tub-like car that spun freely on its way down a serpentine track. The ride was named for ride designer Henry Riehl's daughter, Luna Virginia Riehl. A similar ride was located in Coney Island's Luna Park. (Courtesy of Dan Pisark.)

The Tunnels of Love dark ride was located on the Bowery at West Twelfth Street during the 1920s. The name "Tunnel of Love" was a registered trademark, so the owner added an "s" to "Tunnel" to avoid infringement. The ride was part scenic railway and part dark ride, with strange tableaux, including a scale model of Vatican City. (Courtesy of Charles Denson Archive.)

A c. 1921 view shows Jones Walk with Koster's hotel in the foreground. The Garms family summer home was located in the structure below the Wheel. The Virginia Reel, the Tunnels of Love, and Jackman's Thriller are to the right. Chimneys from Stauch's baths rise in the distance. (Courtesy of Charles Denson Archive.)

A scene on West Twelfth Street in 1924 shows the Wheel behind a primitive structure housing a game. When Thompson Walk was widened and converted to West Twelfth Street in 1923, automobile access to the Wheel became easier. (Courtesy of Charles Denson Archive.)

The 1948 Bowery fire, above, and the 1933 fire on West Twelfth Street, below, came perilously close to the Wonder Wheel but were put down before the Wheel was damaged. Additional fires in 1976 and 1985 destroyed many of the large wooden buildings on Jones Walk. (Both, courtesy of Coney Island History Project.)

A dapper young Freddie Garms, at right, takes a seat on Jones Walk. The walk, owned by the Ward family, resembled a smaller version of the Bowery and was lined with independently operated attractions. Before the boardwalk was built, Jones Walk connected Surf Avenue to Ward's bathhouse and the beach. (Courtesy of Coney Island History Project.)

Walter Kerner Sr., wearing a suit, balances on a narrow platform while changing the bulbs in the Wonder Wheel's sign. Maintenance was usually done without a hardhat or tether. (Courtesy of Kerner family.)

Pictured from left to right, Al Kerner, Walter Kerner Sr., and Albert Kerner pose in front of the Wonder Wheel in the 1940s. German immigrant Albert Kerner married into the Garms family and was a partner in the Wheel from the beginning. His son, Walter, later partnered with Freddie Garms to attain full ownership of the ride in 1970. (Courtesy of Kerner family.)

The 25th-anniversary celebration dinner for the Wonder Wheel shareholders was held in 1945. Most attendees were family members, employees, and local businesspeople who had purchased or been given stock during the difficult construction years. (Courtesy of Hermann family.)

Freddie Garms, in his Army uniform, is in the second row from top; his wife, Barbara, is to the left of him. To the right of him are his mother, Greta, and his father, Herman. Members of the Hermann and Kerner families are seated in the rows at right below the flag. Other family shareholders and employees in attendance included the Schluters, Barbieris, and Kutners. (Courtesy of Herman family.)

Albert Kerner and Anna Garms Kerner are pictured at the Wonder Wheel in 1960. An early version of Spook-A-Rama can be seen in the background, dwarfed by the soon-to-be demolished Feltman's powerplant behind it. (Courtesy of Kerner family.)

Pictured from left to right, Wonder Wheel owner Herman Garms, Anna Kerner, and Greta Garms enjoy a libation in the kitchen of their summer home below the Wonder Wheel in 1957. Freddie Garms, who was known for his love of Chivas Regal scotch, would continue this tradition until his retirement. (Courtesy of Kerner family.)

A 1930s postcard shows the West Twelfth Street entranceway to the Wonder Wheel. Compared to the elaborate neon signage of the 1950s, the painted sign is quite primitive. Column supports for the Virginia Reel can be seen at the left. Because the Wheel was set back from the street, signage with arrows pointing the way to the entrance was necessary. (Courtesy of Coney Island History Project.)

A 1952 image at the ticket booth shows the Wonder Wheel crew in front below a sign offering a $100 bond to the "10th million customer." The Wheel was celebrating its 32nd year of operation. Freddie Garms is at left. Paul Kleinstein, who operated Spook-A-Rama, is at top right, and in front of him is Wonder Wheel owner Herman Garms. Sitting on the ground in the middle is Louis Mintz, the Wheel's main operator. The Wonder Wheel loading platform and maze are behind them. (Courtesy of Coney Island History Project.)

A "thrilling" advertisement from a 1940s Coney Island Chamber of Commerce publication listed the Wheel's statistics and breathlessly declared the ride to be "stupendous!" as well as "a mighty monument to modern engineering." The delightful "dips" refer to the Wheel's original name, Dip the Dip. (Courtesy of Coney Island History Project.)

Until the 1940s, the Bowery connected to the Feltman's Restaurant property and West Tenth Street. A lawsuit initiated by the Ward family against the Feltman family led to the permanent closure of the Bowery connection to Feltman's at Jones Walk. The lawsuit also settled a decades-long easement dispute for all properties along the Bowery. The photograph below shows the closed-off Feltman's entrance and the Wonder Wheel sign around 1948. (Both, courtesy of Charles Denson Archive.)

This stereoview from the Steeplechase pier around 1925 shows a crowded beach and the new boardwalk, completed in 1923. The ornate Stauch's Baths building is at left, and behind it is the Wonder Wheel. At center is the Giant Racer roller coaster on West Tenth Street, soon to be replaced by the Cyclone roller coaster in 1927. Coney Island stereoviews were extremely popular in the 19th century, and this view is one of the last produced. (Courtesy of Charles Denson Archive.)

Ward's baths offered steam rooms, showers, swimsuit rentals, and a rolling chair concession. In the off-season, when the chairs were not being rolled down the boardwalk, they could be rented for sunbathing. (Courtesy of Charles Denson Archive.)

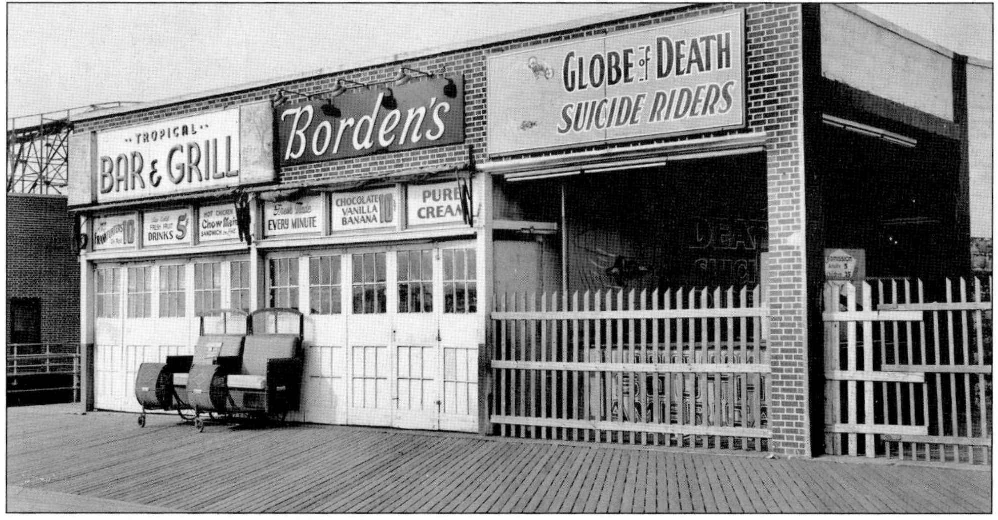

Attractions at Ward's boardwalk establishment changed from year to year. In this image, the bathhouse entrance has been closed and replaced by the Globe of Death Suicide Riders, a motorcycle motordrome. (Courtesy of Charles Denson Archive.)

Charles Hermann's last amusement invention was a giant steel orb called the GyroGlobe. The colorful orb was located on West Twelfth Street opposite the Wonder Wheel and was operated by "Ride King" Jimmy Kryimes, who also had the Looper, Boomerang, Cuddleup, and Virginia Reel. Hermann built the GyroGlobe and was president of Gyro Amusements when the ride was installed in 1947. The company was not a big moneymaker. (Courtesy of Coney Island History Project.)

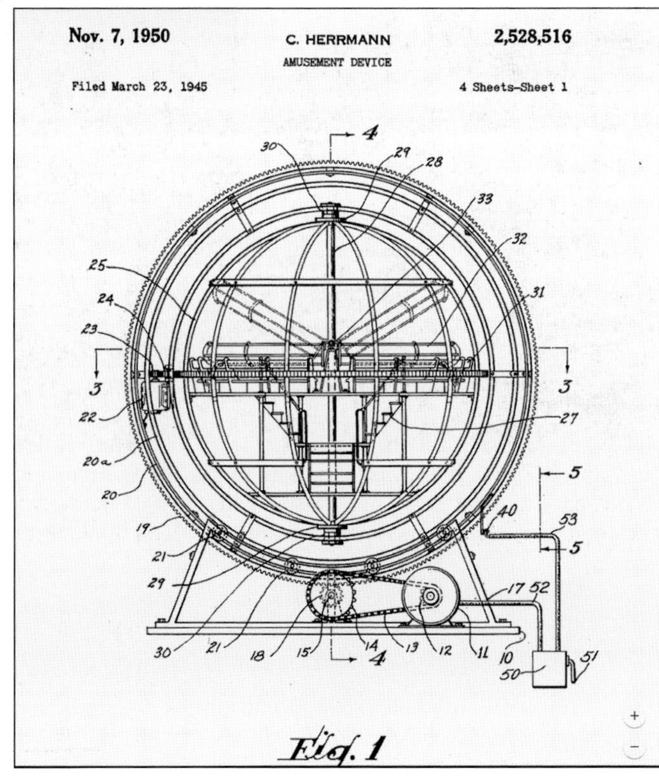

Hermann's 1945 patent for the GyroGlobe was approved in 1950, but his last Coney Island business venture had already gone bankrupt in 1949. (Courtesy of Coney Island History Project.)

"It Spins, It Turns, It Thrills," read a dramatic advertisement for the GyroGlobe. The beautifully lit ride got a lot of attention on West Twelfth Street but few riders. The ride's spectacular lighting became a popular subject for time-exposure photography. (Courtesy of Coney Island History Project.)

In the 1950s, the entrance to Ward's bathhouse was moved to this location on West Twelfth Street below the Wonder Wheel. Today, the storefronts are occupied by the Coney Island History Project, Benny Harrison's games, and his popular Miss Coney Island, an animated dancing robot. The bathhouse frontage on the boardwalk was demolished and converted into Ward's Kiddie Park. (Courtesy of Charles Denson Archive.)

Clarabell, the mute clown from Buffalo Bob's *Howdy Doody* television show, made an appearance at Ward's Kiddie Park and took a ride on the pony carts around 1952. A young Jack Ward, whose family owned the park, stands at bottom left holding cotton candy. The carousel was disassembled and its horses sold to Walt Disney in 1955. (Courtesy of Coney Island History Project.)

Ward's Kiddie Park was just being established when this photograph was taken from the Wonder Wheel in the early 1950s. The carousel and the whip ride were the main attractions. (Courtesy of Coney Island History Project.)

From left to right are Wonder Wheel owners Herman Garms, Walter Kerner, Anna Kerner, Freddie Garms, and Greta Garms. The photograph was taken in the house below the Wonder Wheel. Although the house below the Thunderbolt roller coaster in the movie *Annie Hall* seemed unusual, it was common practice for ride owners to have their summer homes below their establishments. (Courtesy of Kerner family.)

Louie Gargiulo enjoys a drink with Walter Kerner at the Wonder Wheel office in 1976. Gargiulo was the founder of Gargiulo's Restaurant, a popular eatery on West Fifteenth Street, and a regular visitor for happy hour at the Garms summer home. (Courtesy of Kerner family.)

Freddie Garms does what he enjoyed most: climbing around on the Wheel and posing for news cameras during the annual safety inspection by the city's building department around 1950. He never fell from the Wheel, but his father, Herman, survived several falls. (Courtesy of Richard Garms.)

This aerial shot shows Coney Island in the 1930s. West Sixteenth Street and Bushman's Baths are in the foreground. Above that is Stillwell Avenue with Stauch's bathhouse and the narrow Tornado roller coaster. The serpentine tracks of the Virginia Reel are just to the left of the Wonder Wheel, which appears ghostly white. The Bowery is at left, leading up to the heavily wooded Feltman Bavarian Village on West Tenth Street. Two roller coasters side by side at top are the 1927 Cyclone and the 1921 Wildcat. The long, narrow structures throughout the photograph are wooden bathhouse lockers and rooms. The open rooftop deck on top of the Stauch's building just below the Tornado was used for nude sunbathing. (Courtesy of Charles Denson Archive.)

This corner of the Bowery and West Twelfth Street changed dramatically when Ward's block-long Scoota-Boat ride was demolished in the late 1940s. A Whirl-A-Way ride opened on the site and operated there for a decade. (Courtesy of Coney Island History Project.)

CONEY ISLAND
WONDER WHEEL

* * *

East Side, West Side,
All around the town,
New Yorker's seek their pleasure,
As they ride aroun' an' 'roun.

Young and old enjoy it,
Millions ride and feel
The thrill on the—STUPENDOUS!
CONEY ISLAND - WONDER WHEEL!

* * *

WEL - COME! TOUR - ISTS,
To our great, big town.
Take in its star attractions,
On your pleasure trip aroun'.

The WORLD'S AMUSEMENT SKY - RIDE
Has got the thrill ideal.
Go up! It's great! - COLOSSAL!
CONEY ISLAND - WONDER WHEEL!

* * *

Let's Go! - Up - Now!
And from high look down,
Upon the Wonder City,
Seen for miles an' miles aroun'.

Boys and girls and grown-ups,
All get a thrill that's real,
Upon the GREAT! - GIGANTIC!
CONEY ISLAND - WONDER WHEEL!

* * *

The "thrilling" Wonder Wheel provided inspiration for songwriters and poets, as expressed in this sweet 1920s song. (Courtesy of Kerner family.)

! ! ! ! ! ! !

SEASON PASS — Good Only During Year —

This Pass is Not Transferable

Issued subject to conditions on back hereof

WONDER WHEEL

World's Largest Ride!

! ! !

52 JONES WALK

BET. BOARDWALK AND BOWERY

! ! !

CONEY ISLAND, NEW YORK CITY

! ! !

MILLION AMUSEMENT CORP.

OPERATING LICENSEE

Not Good Sat., Sun. and Holidays

Free Tickets Issued as Punched Below

No.

TICKET(S) ISSUED

(See back hereof)

1	2	3	4	5	6

This 1950s season pass for the Wonder Wheel was issued by Million Amusement Corporation. (Courtesy of Coney Island History Project.)

BOOMERANG
BOWERY & W. 12th ST.
CONEY ISLAND
ADMIT ONE 20¢
B 12031

HURRICANE RIDE
Bowery & W. 12th St.
Coney Island, N. Y.
ADMIT ONE 20¢
B 30105

MOTOR PARKWAY
BOWERY & 12th STREET
CONEY ISLAND, N. Y.
ADMIT ONE
TOTAL
EST. PRICE .19
NYC TAX - .01
20c
058297

Wonder Wheel
CONEY ISLAND, N.Y.
ADMIT ONE
1.00
$1.00 PRICE $1.00
INCLUDES TAX
GLOBE TICKET COMPANY (S) 260
018172

These tickets from West Twelfth Street attractions show the variety of amusements that lined the street over the years. Most of the rides were owned by Mike Curran or Jimmy Kryimes, who also owned the Virginia Reel. Charles Hermann's GyroGlobe would join the lineup in the 1940s before moving to Long Beach, California. (Courtesy of Coney Island History Project.)

An animated Cyclops loomed over a small waterfall at the Bowery entrance to Spook-A-Rama in 1970. Another Cyclops was located farther up Jones Walk next to the Wheel. Monster movies of the 1950s provided the main themes for the ride. The Cyclops is now on exhibit at the Coney Island History Project. (Photograph by Charles Denson.)

Artist Dan Casola never received proper credit for the bizarre artwork he created at the Wonder Wheel's Spook-A-Rama dark ride. He preferred to remain anonymous. Like the builders of the Wonder Wheel, Casola was an immigrant, born in Italy as the son of a shoemaker. His work spanned the entire frontage of Jones Walk. All of the animated figures, murals, menus, and decorative signs were created in his workshop behind the ride. His collectible sideshow banners now sell for tens of thousands of dollars. (Courtesy of Casola family.)

One of Casola's mural sections was removed from Spook-A-Rama years ago and is now in a private collection. This work was shown in several museums, including the Brooklyn Museum, the Wadsworth Atheneum, the San Diego Museum of Art, and the McNay Art Museum in San Antonio. The creature at the bottom has a warning to "keep feet & hands inside of car." Casola's twisted sense of humor was often displayed in his signage. (Courtesy of Coney Island History Project.)

Casola created works for many Coney Island attractions, including this rotating, fire-breathing creature he built for the entrance to the Dragon's Cave dark ride on the Bowery. He also made many of the figures in the World of Wax museum on Stillwell Avenue. (Courtesy of Casola family.)

During the Watergate hearings of the 1970s, a topical sign above the entrance to Spook-A-Rama challenged people to "Ride the Watergate," a reference to the simulated waterfall at the Bowery entrance to the ride. (Courtesy of Casola family.)

In 1968, Dan Casola posed in front of his creations with his daughter, Patricia, second from right, and her friends. Above them are his animated figures of Laurel and Hardy and some of Casola's bizarre menu signs. Many of these stored Casola artworks are unearthed and displayed at the Wonder Wheel's annual History Day. (Courtesy of Casola family.)

Freddie Garms holds court at Ward's Boardwalk Kiddie Park shortly before he sold the Wonder Wheel to Denos Vourderis. Vourderis, who is standing in the background, was the manager of the park before he bought the Wheel in 1983. Even after he sold the Wheel, Garms remained involved in Coney Island and was president of the Coney Island Chamber of Commerce. (Courtesy of Deno's Wonder Wheel.)

Freddie Garms, at left, wrote on the back of this Polaroid photo: "History is made 6/14/73. The first female to ride on top of a swinging car—Pat Fox." Garms enjoyed performing dangerous stunts on the wheel, including climbing all over it without a harness or restraints of any kind. Pat Fox seems a little nervous, or perhaps dazed. Despite stunts like this the Wheel has maintained a perfect safety record since 1920. (Courtesy of Deno's Wonder Wheel.)

Pat Fox and an unidentified worker paint the cast iron targets at the park's Jones Walk shooting gallery in 1973. (Courtesy of Deno's Wonder Wheel.)

An aerial view shows the variety of rides and attractions along the beach and boardwalk at Coney Island around 1963. The Wonder Wheel is at left, and below it are the attractions on Ward's Jones Walk property that would be destroyed by fire in 1985. Just below the Wheel is the house that the Garms family lived in during the summer. The curving tracks of the Virginia Reel run from the Bowery to the base of the Wheel. Along West Twelfth Street to the right of the Reel's sign are Charles Hermann's GyroGlobe ride and the Himalaya. At lower center are the Paratrooper and Roundup and an assortment of Jimmy McCullough's rides located on the Bowery. The substantial brick building at the bottom is the Coney Island Bank, and to its right is the 1917 Childs Restaurant Building on Surf Avenue. The two large roller coasters are the Tornado (left)

on Stillwell Avenue and the Thunderbolt (right). Squeezed between them is the Bobsled coaster. Stauch's Bathhouse, a beautiful terra-cotta palace, is below the Seagram's billboard. Two famous landmarks, the Steeplechase Pier and the Parachute Jump, are situated at the beach. A corner of the Steeplechase Pavilion is just to the right of the Parachute Jump. The Wonder Wheel is the only ride in this photograph that is still operating. Nearly all of the structures were lost to various fires over the years. The pier survived several fires and was rebuilt after being heavily damaged in Hurricane Sandy in 2012. Steeplechase Park was demolished in 1966. (Courtesy of Coney Island History Project.)

This view from the boardwalk looks down West Twelfth Street in 1970. The large gas tank in the background belonged to Brooklyn Union Gas Company and was situated on Coney Island Creek. (Photograph by Charles Denson.)

In this 1970 photograph, the spirals of a toboggan ride on West Twelfth Street appear to be part of the Wonder Wheel. A banner on the Wheel announces its 50th anniversary. (Courtesy of Deno's Wonder Wheel.)

A 1970 view from the subway shows the historic Grashorn Building, Coney Island's oldest, and the Wonder Wheel in the background. Jones Walk is to the left. The Sky Ride at Astroland is at left. Henry Grashorn's hardware store once provided all the amusements with hard-to-find parts. (Courtesy of Abe Feinstein.)

Mr. Garms and Mr. Kerner advised the corporation that they had contracted to purchase from Wonder Wheel, Inc., incorporated January 26, 1920 (now dissolved), for the sum of $62,000.00, the amusement device known as the "wonder wheel" together with its equipment, parts, tools and all other personal property of whatsoever kind and nature used or intended to be used in connection with the operation, repair and maintenance of the amusement device, the right to the name "Wonder Wheel, Inc." and any and all copyrights thereof, together with the right to incorporate a new corporation to be known as "Wonder Wheel, Inc.", as well as the right, title and interest of the former corporation in and to its tenancy of the real property located at Jones Walk, Coney Island, upon which the amusement device and appurtenant structures are situated. Mr. Garms and Mr. Kerner offered to cause the various interests to be sold and transferred directly to this

In 1970, Freddie Garms and Walter Kerner bought the Wonder Wheel and all of its equipment from its shareholders for $62,000. Thirteen years later, the partnership sold the Wheel to Denos Vourderis for $250,000, and he spent the same amount repairing it. (Courtesy of Kerner family.)

Denos Vourderis poses at the entrance ramp to the Wonder Wheel, his proud new possession, shortly after becoming the new owner. (Courtesy of Deno's Wonder Wheel.)

Three

Deno's Wonder Wheel Park

Greek immigrant Denos Vourderis recalled the promise he made to his girlfriend Lula in 1948. "I told her, 'You marry me, I buy you the Wonder Wheel,'" he said. "I couldn't buy it because I had no money. I bought her two wheels instead, a pushcart!" But Lula married him anyway, and 35 years later, the one-time hot-dog peddler kept his promise and bought her the Wonder Wheel, the world's largest engagement ring.

The summer of 1983 was not a good time to buy a Coney Island business, and many longtime operators were giving up and moving on, fleeing the area. But Denos believed that Coney Island had a bright future and decided to follow his dream. "Our whole life has been a gamble," Lula told a reporter in 1987, "Denos is a workaholic, and if he makes up his mind, nobody can change it."

Denos's life played out like a novel, and the twists and turns that led to his founding of Deno's Wonder Wheel Park at Coney Island are legendary. He was born Constantinos Dionysios Vourderis in Aigion, Greece, the eighth of 22 children. The year of his birth was 1920, the same year that the Wonder Wheel was constructed. After joining the merchant marine in Greece at 14 and being trained as a cook, he jumped ship in Baltimore in 1939. Denos gained American citizenship by joining the US Army and serving with distinction in World War II, earning the Good Conduct Medal, Meritorious Unit Award, American Theater Ribbon, and World War II Victory Ribbon before being honorably discharged in June 1946.

Following the war, returning veterans were made eligible for New York City peddler's licenses, and Denos began operating a hot-dog pushcart in upper Manhattan near Columbia University and City College. Later, he would joke about his lack of education: "If I could read, I'd be richer than Rockefeller." He loved the food business but was also mechanically inclined and began a side business of appliance repair, a skill that would later help him build his amusement park.

The couple had ambitions beyond pushcarts and opened their first restaurant in Tarrytown, New York, in the early 1950s. Later, they moved to Astoria, Queens, and opened another restaurant. By the 1960s, they had opened two more restaurants and had four children, Dennis, Steve, Aristea, and Helen.

Vourderis had always loved visiting Coney Island, and in 1966, he received an offer he couldn't refuse: the management and lease of the Anchor Bar and Grill, a small restaurant on the boardwalk behind the Cyclone roller coaster. It was there that he learned the rough, fast-paced business world of Coney Island.

By the summer of 1969, the Anchor Bar had suffered an arson fire started by burglars during a break-in, and soon after that, the entire building was taken by the city through eminent domain to expand the adjacent New York Aquarium.

Denos needed a new venue and found it a block away at Ward's Kiddie Park. He told Ward's manager, John Curran, that a food concession was lacking at his park. Curran invited him to bring in a small food stand. Curran and the Wards were impressed with the competence and ambition of the Vourderis family and allowed them to build a larger restaurant building on the property. In 1980, John Curran retired and sold Ward's Kiddie Park to Denos for no money down and four payments of $37,500, which Denos paid off during his next four summers of operation. The tiny, colorful original food stand that Denos built at the park remains in operation today.

A few years after purchasing the Kiddie Park, Denos got a call from Freddie Garms, whose family had owned and operated the Wonder Wheel since 1920. Garms wanted to retire and sell the Wheel, but he only knew one person who could maintain it and keep it running. "He asked me for $250,000," Denos remembered, "and I said, 'You got it!' "

Garms had received other offers to buy the Wheel, including from buyers who wanted to move it out of Coney Island, but he knew that Denos was the only one who could care for it. The sale offer included the iconic Spook-A-Rama dark ride and the games on Jones Walk. Dennis Vourderis, Denos's son, was apprehensive about the deal and worried about getting into debt so soon after buying the Kiddie Park.

"You got too much education and no guts," Denos told his son. "You analyze too much. If I had your brains I'd never be where I am now." Dennis remembers his father saying, "I know this place will be better, it has to be." Dennis added, "And you know what, he was right!"

Shortly before the sale was completed, Denos was stabbed in the chest during an altercation with a homeless man at the park. He was in the hospital when his children asked him to reconsider the purchase, but he would have none of it. Denos recovered from his injury and became the owner of Coney Island's most incredible ride. The venture was so successful that he paid off the debt in less than two years. Four years after purchasing the Wheel, Denos bought all the property under the Wheel and along Jones Walk from the Ward family for nearly $1 million and began piecing together what would become Coney Island's newest attraction: Deno's Wonder Wheel Park.

When the Vourderis family took over the venerable Wheel, it had fallen into disrepair and needed a complete overhaul. Steve and Dennis were put in charge of the enormous job of restoring the structure to its former glory. There was no owner's manual, and the only written instructions were scrawled on an old piece of cardboard, a confusing list that ended with the words "Good Luck." After a backbreaking restoration that took several years, the Wonder Wheel prospered, becoming an official New York City landmark in 1989.

Three generations of the Vourderis family—parents, children, and grandchildren—have worked to make Deno's Wonder Wheel Park a success story, the best that Coney Island has to offer. Denos passed away in 1994, and Lula followed him in 2019. Setbacks including fires and hurricanes have not dampened the Coney Island spirit of this remarkable family, and the new generation has expanded the park, adding many new attractions while preserving the classics. It now boasts 16 rides in the kiddie park and five major adult rides, including a restored Spook-A-Rama and a new 7D virtual reality attraction. In 2019, the Vourderis family purchased a large adjacent property and revealed plans to expand the park, ensuring that the next generation is ready for the future.

Denos Vourderis, center, learned to cook after joining the merchant marine in Greece at 14. Here he sets up a spread on a ship at sea, where he honed the skills he would need for his future food businesses. (Courtesy of Deno's Wonder Wheel.)

Denos Vourderis is "on safari" in a photo studio. Fighting tigers was easy work compared to running a business in Coney Island. (Courtesy of Deno's Wonder Wheel.)

Returning World War II veterans were eligible for New York City peddler's licenses, and Denos Vourderis received one to operate an ice cream truck and later a sidewalk hot-dog cart. Vourderis, still in uniform, poses with his new car next to a line of ice cream trucks in 1946. (Courtesy of Deno's Wonder Wheel.)

Denos Vourderis sharpens a knife as he prepares a meal on the deck of a ship during his stint as a merchant marine cook around 1939. (Courtesy of Deno's Wonder Wheel.)

Denos and Lula Vourderis are pictured at their restaurant in Queens, New York. The couple would open four diners during the 1950s. (Courtesy of Deno's Wonder Wheel.)

Denos Vourderis and his then-girlfriend Lula are pictured on the beach at Coney Island around 1947. When he proposed, he told Lula that he didn't have enough money for a ring, but if she married him, he would buy her the Wonder Wheel as a wedding gift. She accepted, and he kept his promise. (Courtesy of Deno's Wonder Wheel.)

Lula and Denos Vourderis were married in 1948. Lula was born in New York but spent her childhood in Greece. She lost her mother when she was six years old and grew up with great deprivation during World War II. The family moved back to New York after the war, and Lula worked with her father selling hot dogs from a pushcart. (Courtesy of Deno's Wonder Wheel.)

The Anchor Bar and Grill was the first business that Denos Vourderis had in Coney Island. The building was gutted in a 1968 arson fire started by a burglar, and it was later taken by the city through eminent domain and made part of the New York Aquarium. The structure now houses the aquarium's education hall. (Courtesy of Deno's Wonder Wheel.)

A still from a home movie shows Denos Vourderis at the food counter of the Anchor Bar and Grill wearing his gold-colored catering jacket. (Courtesy of Coney Island History Project.)

Denos Vourderis is interviewed by a reporter outside his boardwalk snack bar in the 1970s. A tireless Coney Island promoter, he never doubted that the best days for the resort were ahead. (Courtesy of Deno's Wonder Wheel.)

Ward's Kiddie Park and carousel on the boardwalk are pictured before Denos Vourderis took over ownership in the 1980. The Kiddie Park was built on the boardwalk level of the old Ward's bathhouse after the structure's upper floors were removed in the early 1950s. Ride tickets were advertised as 9¢, allowing for a penny tax to avoid having to make change for a dime. (Courtesy of Coney Island History Project.)

An ecstatic Denos Vourderis (left) toasts Freddie Garms on the day he closed the deal to purchase the Wonder Wheel. Not only had he survived a life-threatening stabbing attack, but he had also finally fulfilled the promise he made to his wife, Lula, in 1948. During the next 11 years, Denos and Lula would continue to invest in Coney Island, acquire property, and buy new and exciting rides for the establishment he christened Deno's Wonder Wheel Park. (Courtesy of Deno's Wonder Wheel.)

Shortly after purchasing the Wonder Wheel in 1983, Denos and sons Steve (left) and Dennis (center) pondered the enormous amount of work needed to keep the Wheel going. Steve, a trained airplane mechanic, was in charge of the Wheel's restoration as well as repairing and maintaining the park's other rides. (Courtesy of Deno's Wonder Wheel.)

Lula Vourderis, the family matriarch, was a kind woman who never forgot her difficult childhood in Greece during World War II. She fed everyone, including the homeless. "After going hungry, she took joy in feeding people, even if they couldn't pay," her grandson D.J. said. "Visitors came to the park for Lula's shish kebab, fried shrimp, and cotton candy. Everybody called her mom because she fed everybody." Lula was a constant and reassuring presence in the park until she passed away in 2019. (Courtesy of Deno's Wonder Wheel.)

World War II veteran Denos Vourderis salutes paratroopers on the beach during a Coney Island air show in the 1980s. Deno's Wonder Wheel Park, Astroland, and the Coney Island Chamber of Commerce were the main sponsors of these popular events. (Courtesy of Deno's Wonder Wheel.)

The upbeat greeting displayed on the Deno's Snack Bar awning reads "DENO SEZ Welcome to Coney Island." In 1976, the entire Vourderis family worked together to build this structure at Ward's Kiddie Park on the boardwalk. As Coney Island fell on hard times, Denos Vourderis always believed that the neighborhood would recover and return to its former glory. His risks paid off, as his park become an anchor of Coney Island. (Courtesy of Deno's Wonder Wheel.)

Steve Vourderis inspects the Wonder Wheel hub shortly after the family purchased the venerable ride in 1983. The ride had years of deferred maintenance, and he and his brother, Dennis, had to work at repairing and replacing much of the Wheel's structure, including jacking up the hub to replace the rollers. Roller replacement can take several days and involves jacking up the 150-ton wheel at the axle and installing nine new 90-pound machined rollers. (Courtesy of Deno's Wonder Wheel.)

Deno's Wonder Wheel Park manager Reggie Pryor cleans and welds one of the Wheel's car carriages shortly after the Vourderis family bought the ride. (Courtesy of Deno's Wonder Wheel.)

This worn roller in the Wonder Wheel's hub is pictured just before it was replaced in 1984. (Courtesy of Deno's Wonder Wheel.)

The Wonder Wheel did not come with an operating manual. Walter Kerner provided the Vourderis family a set of scrawled instructions on the inside of an old cigarette carton. A simplified tip says that to lift the wheel "loosen all nuts and see if bolts move and retighten." The final line says "Good Luck." (Courtesy of Deno's Wonder Wheel.)

Jorge "Chico" Gallegos works high atop the Wheel's hub, which has to be stripped and repainted every winter, a cold and unforgiving job. Every 10 years, the 90-pound rollers have to be replaced. A newly machined roller is at right. (Photographs by Charles Denson.)

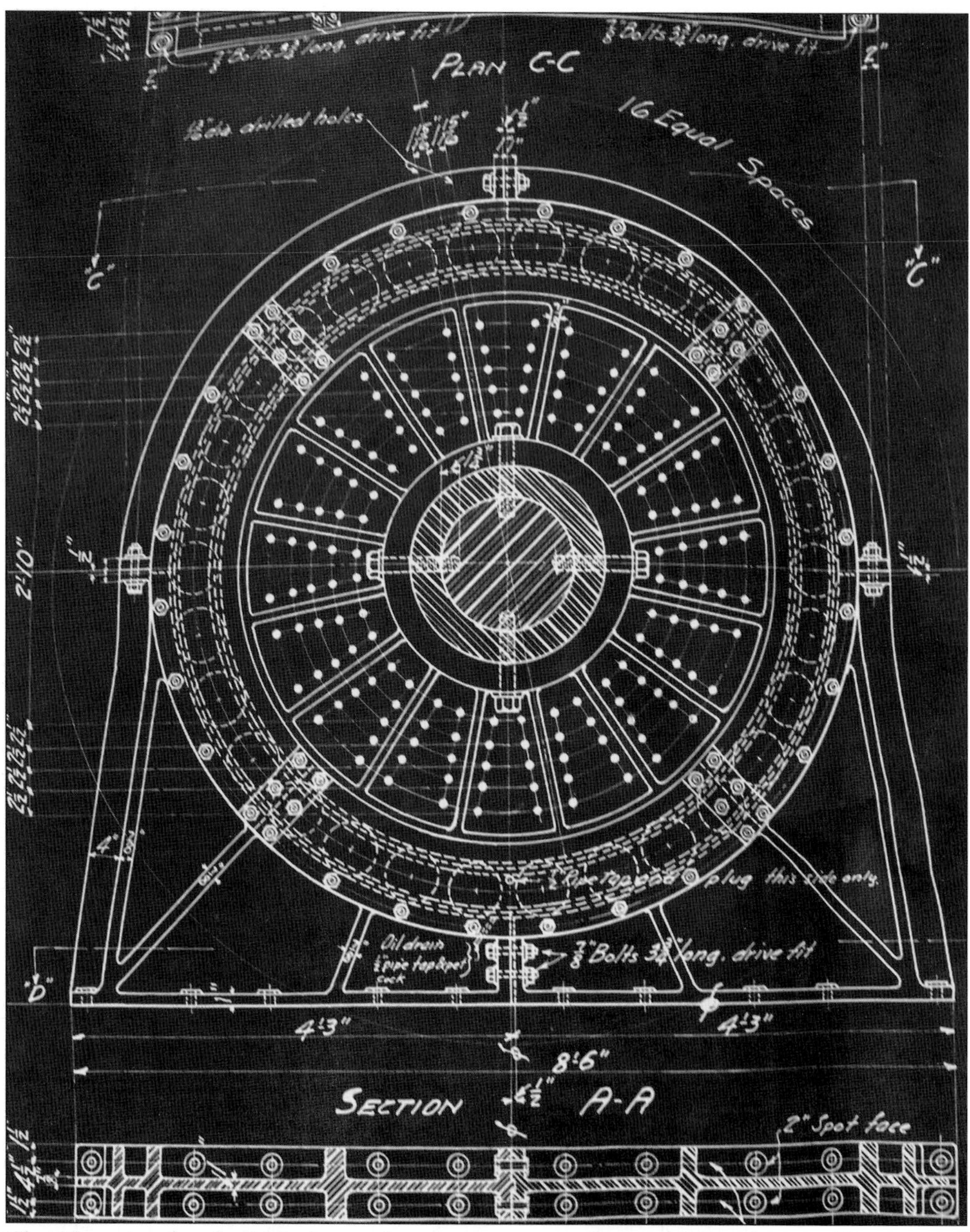

The blueprint for the hub shows the enormous complexity of the design. (Courtesy of Deno's Wonder Wheel.)

This dizzying and unusual view was taken from the hub of the Wonder Wheel. The hub is accessed via a ladder on one of the Wheel's four legs. Made from high-quality Bethlehem steel, the century-old axle bears 150 tons of weight and must be kept constantly lubricated. (Photograph by Charles Denson.)

On January 31, 1985, a devastating fire destroyed all the amusement buildings on Jones Walk between the Bowery and the Wonder Wheel. The Wheel was scorched and lost most of its neon spokes. Spook-A-Rama was also heavily damaged. The ride, which was advertised as the "longest spook ride in the world," was shortened after the fire, and the Bowery entrance was replaced with concessions. This photograph shows the Bowery cleared of debris before the Vourderis family bought the property from the Wards and added it to the park. (Courtesy of Coney Island History Project.)

The location today shows a revitalized Bowery and the entrance to Deno's at right. The Bowl-Oh-Rama game is in the space occupied by Spook-A-Rama before the 1985 fire. (Photograph by Charles Denson.)

The corner of West Twelfth Street and the Bowery has had a changing face for more than a century. Attractions once at this location include a hotel, the Tunnels of Love, the Looper, the Scoota-Boat Ride, Pony Rides, and the Cortina Bob, above, which ran through the 1970s. The Vourderis family operated their Pizza Palace stand on the corner in the 1980s. In 2019, the family bought the entire parcel, from the Bowery to the Wonder Wheel, for an expansion of Deno's Wonder Wheel Park. (Courtesy of Coney Island History Project.)

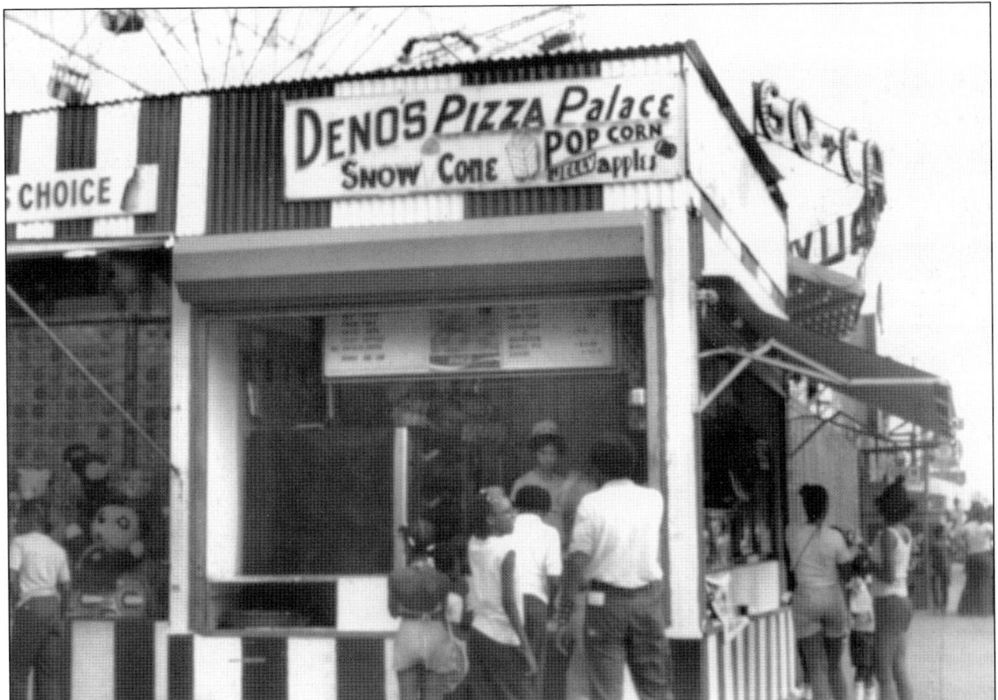

Restaurants were the main business of the Vourderis family for several decades. At one time, the family had three food stands on West Twelfth Street adjacent to the Wonder Wheel. (Courtesy of Deno's Wonder Wheel.)

Members of the Vourderis family gathered for a photograph shortly after they purchased the Wonder Wheel. From left to right are (first row) Teddy, Stacy, John, and Deno "D.J."; (second row) Steve, Dennis, Lula, Helen, Daniel LaChase, Denos, and Aristea LaChase. (Courtesy of Deno's Wonder Wheel.)

Attorney Jack Ward, William J. Ward's grandson, was one of Coney Island's boosters and leaders. He was president of the Coney Island Chamber of Commerce and managed the family's Coney Island properties, which dated back to the original 1800s land grants. His law office had once been located in Manhattan's World Trade Center, but he decided to return to his Coney Island roots and moved back in 2000, shortly before the towers were attacked, a move that may have saved his life. (Photograph by Charles Denson.)

In 2008, the Coney Island History Project inducted the Ward family into the Coney Island Hall of Fame. Jack and his wife, Mary Beth, accepted the award from Coney Island History Project executive director Charles Denson. Ward passed away in 2011 at the age of 66. (Courtesy of Coney Island History Project.)

Neon is the main lighting around the Wonder Wheel, and two signs on the Bowery and on West Twelfth Street are classics. The rose-colored neon spokes used to be removed every winter to avoid damage from ice, but now the neon remains on year-round, as more spokes were damaged by removal than by ice. (Photographs by Charles Denson.)

In 2010, D.J. Vourderis designed and built a system of solar panels for the roofs of the Wonder Wheel cars. Batteries in each car powered the decorative lights that were part of the original design. The entire innovative system was destroyed by Hurricane Sandy in 2012 and has not been replaced. (Photographs by Charles Denson.)

The scary eyeball doors at the entrance to Spook-A-Rama are the work of Dan Casola and remain as part of the original design. A tremendous bang of the doors scares riders as the cars enter and leave the spook-house. (Photograph by Charles Denson.)

Deno's Wonder Wheel Park has a vast collection of classic and new technology, including the popular Stop the Zombies! 7D virtual reality attraction on the park's Jones Walk midway. (Photograph by Charles Denson.)

A fight and chase scene in the 1985 MGM movie *Remo Williams: The Adventure Begins* included a stuntman dangling from one of the Wonder Wheel's cars, something that Freddie Garms could probably do with ease. (Courtesy of Deno's Wonder Wheel.)

Actor Fred Ward poses with members of the Vourderis family during a break in the *Remo Williams* filming. From left to right are Helen, Stacy, Fred Ward, Denos, and D.J. (Courtesy of Deno's Wonder Wheel.)

Actress Helen Hunt took a break from filming for a ride on the Wheel and a visit with Vourderis family members (from left to right) Timothy, Nicholas, Denos, and Dennis. (Courtesy of Deno's Wonder Wheel.)

Ted Danson (left) and D.J. Vourderis are pictured at the Wonder Wheel during the filming of the HBO comedy series *Bored to Death*. Other actors who have been filmed on the Wheel include Beyoncé, Christian Slater, Rami Malek, and Jennifer Lopez. (Photograph by Charles Denson.)

A live tiger takes a spin on the Wonder Wheel during the filming of a pilot for the television show *NYPD Mounted*. The series was later renamed *NYPD Blue*. (Courtesy of Deno's Wonder Wheel.)

Actor Mickey Rourke walks the Coney Island beach in the 1987 film *Angel Heart*. (Courtesy of Deno's Wonder Wheel.)

In 2001, the City of New York honored Denos Vourderis by renaming West Twelfth Street Denos D. Vourderis Place. The street sign is on the boardwalk next to the Wonder Wheel. (Photograph by Jim McDonnell.)

The Vourderis family gathered at the Boardwalk for the 2001 street-naming ceremony honoring Denos Vourderis. Lula Vourderis stands just to the left of the sign honoring her late husband. Denos passed away in 1994. (Courtesy of Deno's Wonder Wheel.)

Steve (left) and Dennis Vourderis are pictured in 2001. The brothers have honored their father's legacy at Deno's Wonder Wheel Park by continuing the charity work with Salt and Sea Mission that he started decades ago. (Photograph by Charles Denson.)

The colorful midway at Deno's Wonder Wheel Park was built on the boardwalk level of the old Ward's bathhouse. (Photograph by Jim McDonell.)

The Wonder Wheel is a true work of art and the subject of many artists and photographers who have captured its magical qualities. A painter sets up his easel on Surf Avenue to paint an abstract portrait of the ride on a hot summer night. The building in front of the Wonder Wheel was William Ward's Bank of Coney Island, built as part of the 1920s Coney Island revival. In 2014, the building was demolished by a real estate speculator. (Photograph by Charles Denson.)

Crowds flocked to Deno's Kiddie Park on Memorial Day 2016. The Kiddie Park has 16 rides, including a tilt-a-whirl, the Sea Serpent roller coaster, a carousel, classic fire engines, pony carts, mini pirate ships, dizzy dragons, big trucks, a Rio Grande train, and the original Deno's Snack Bar, serving funnel cakes and cotton candy. The ramp at left leads to the Wonder Wheel. (Photograph by Charles Denson.)

A history tour brochure guides visitors throughout the park. Numbered plaques point out classic and historic rides and points of interest. This plaque describes the beautiful carousel built by Chance Manufacturing of Wichita, Kansas, a fixture in the park since 1972. (Photograph by Tricia Vita.)

Martin Villacis paints one of the cars after it has been removed from the Wheel and brought to the workshop below the Kiddie Park. Cars are disassembled, repaired, and painted when the season ends, and winter can sometimes be the busiest time of year for the staff. (Photograph by Charles Denson.)

Reggie Pryor tightens a shock absorber spring above the Wheel's swinging cars. (Photograph by Charles Denson.)

Jorge "Chico" Gallegos attaches a swinging car to the Wheel. Installation of the cars is a complicated but fast-moving process. (Photograph by Charles Denson.)

Steve Vourderis lifts a refurbished car onto the Wheel at the beginning of the season. Forklifts have made the process much easier. (Photograph by Charles Denson.)

On May 23, 1989, the Wonder Wheel became an official New York City landmark. The commission's landmark report stated that "the Wheel has come, along with the Parachute Jump, to symbolize Coney Island." (Photograph by Charles Denson.)

This exciting view shows a swinging car shooting down the tracks of the Wonder Wheel. The Wheel gives riders a choice of experiences: a stationary car that travels to the top of the structure, where there is a sweeping panorama of New York City, or a thrilling "roller coaster" ride in a car that gives the illusion of sliding right off the Wheel. (Photograph by Jim McDonnell.)

As Hurricane Sandy approached New York on October 29, 2012, Steve Vourderis secured the Wonder Wheel with winches and steel cables. Deno's Wonder Wheel Park sustained substantial damage from the storm surge. The family worked hard throughout the winter to repair the damage, and the park was able to reopen on time in the spring of 2013. (Photograph by Charles Denson.)

Hurricane Sandy's storm surge flooded sections of the park with up to eight feet of seawater. Much of the park's infrastructure and the machine shops are located below grade and were destroyed. Cleanup and salvage began the following morning. Spook-A-Rama had to be completely rebuilt from the ground up, but the ride's classic cars were saved and restored. Almost none of the arcade games could be saved. (Photograph by Charles Denson.)

All of the solar panels and electronics that powered the lighting on the Wheel's cars were damaged beyond repair by Hurricane Sandy. It took months of work to clear the damaged equipment and bring the park back to life. (Photograph by Charles Denson.)

The park's shop was flooded, and many tools and pieces of machinery had to be replaced after being submerged in saltwater. Steve Vourderis checks an electrical panel during the cleanup. (Photograph by Charles Denson.)

In 2014, the historic Astroland Rocket was moved to Deno's Wonder Wheel Park after it was discovered abandoned by the city on a Staten Island pier. Astroland owner Carol Hill Albert, who had donated the rocket to the city, paid to have it moved back to Coney Island, and the Vourderis family provided a new home for it. (Photograph by Charles Denson.)

A view of the crowded Jones Walk midway at Deno's Wonder Wheel Park shows the entrance to the post-Sandy Spook-A-Rama dark ride at right and the entrance to the Wonder Wheel at left. A white stationary (non-swinging) car rises above the crowd. (Courtesy of Jim McDonnell.)

Seen from the front, the Wonder Wheel seems enormous, but this view from the side shows how thin and delicate the structure actually is. Neon lighting is an important attraction at the Wheel, and this colorful animated sign on West Twelfth Street, with its spinning cars in flashing neon, is a popular and often-photographed beacon. The landmark sign has been damaged many times by trucks backing into it but has been completely restored and updated. (Photographs by Charles Denson.)

Astroland's iconic Astrotower stood beside the Wonder Wheel for half a century. On July 4, 2013, the tower was declared unsafe due to unusual swaying. It was condemned and taken down in an emergency demolition. (Photograph by Charles Denson.)

This is one of the 40-horsepower motors that drives the Wonder Wheel. In the 1920s, Charles Hermann had plans to build a dynamo to power the rides of Coney Island but gave up the idea when Con Edison agreed to replace all of the old DC motors and light bulbs when the utility converted to AC current. (Photograph by Charles Denson.)

The Wheel's control panel, designed by Trekkie D.J. Vourderis, includes a row of nine "warp speed" buttons on the right, a tribute to *Star Trek*. The panel runs off an inverter that converts AC current to DC and then back to AC, enabling the motor to operate at precise speeds and torques. The original, highly inefficient system had AC current regulated by resistors that created a lot of heat. A programmable logic controller (PLC) anticipates any scenario involving the running of the Wheel. This system gives complete control over forward and reverse speeds and compensates for weight and wind shifts. D.J. also designed an "autopilot" system. (Both, courtesy of Deno's Wonder Wheel.)

Deno's Wonder Wheel Park was built around food and family. The tradition continues, as all family members still take turns preparing and serving at the park's culinary concessions. Here, family members take a break at their boardwalk restaurant: (from left to right) Joseph, Denos, Cindy, Nicholas, Timothy, Diane, Fran, Dennis, and Lisa. (Courtesy of Deno's Wonder Wheel.)

Dennis Vourderis takes a turn serving at the Kiddie Park's historic Sweet Shop. (Photograph by Jim McDonnell.)

In 1994, Brooklyn borough president Howard Golden honored the Vourderis family with a proclamation celebrating their longtime charity work with Coney Island's Salt and Sea Mission. The family had just raffled off a car to support the mission's work. From left to right are Denos Vourderis, Salt and Sea Mission director Debbe Santiago, Howard Golden, Dennis Vourderis, and publicist Ken Hochman. (Courtesy of Deno's Wonder Wheel.)

Every Labor Day, dozens of unicyclists participating in the NYC Unicycle Festival ride to Coney Island to pose with their wheels in front of the "Big Wheel." Deno's Wonder Wheel Park is one of the sponsors of this unusual event. (Photograph by Jim McDonnell.)

Ringo the Wonder Dog, the late Wonder Wheel mascot, always liked to ride on the forklift operated by Teddy Vourderis during installation of the cars at the beginning of the season. The Wonder Wheel has a canine tradition dating back to the days when the park's watchdogs were allowed to ride in the cars during the day. (Photograph by Jim McDonell.)

Jimmy Prince and Lula Vourderis are pictured at History Day at the Coney Island History Project in 2011. Prince became a volunteer at the History Project after retiring from a 60-year career running Major's Market on Mermaid Avenue. (Photograph by Charles Denson.)

The Spook-A-Rama Cyclops and an original Steeplechase Park horse are among the artifacts on display at the Coney Island History Project exhibit center, located at the West Twelfth Street entrance to the Wonder Wheel. (Photograph by Tricia Vita.)

From left to right, D.J. Vourderis and his wife, Daniela, are pictured with Stacy Vourderis at History Day in 2019. Stacy's love of history led to the creation of this popular annual event in 2011. She has also saved and preserved the Wonder Wheel's numerous historic artifacts and displays them on History Day. (Photograph by Tricia Vita.)

Local officials and the Vourderis family gather for the annual ribbon-cutting ceremony and "Blessing of the Rides" on opening day at the Wonder Wheel, Palm Sunday 2019. (Photograph by Charles Denson.)

Lula and Denos Vourderis realized the American Dream after he kept his promise to buy her the Wonder Wheel. (Courtesy of Deno's Wonder Wheel.)

The Coney Island History Project exhibit center is located next to the Wonder Wheel on West Twelfth Street. The Coney Island History Project, founded in 2004 by Astroland owners Carol Hill Albert and Jerome Albert, is a 501(c)(3) nonprofit organization that aims to increase awareness of Coney Island's legendary and colorful past and to encourage appreciation of the Coney Island neighborhood of today. The History Project's mission is to record, archive, and share oral history interviews; provide access to historical artifacts and documentary material through educational exhibits, events, and the website www.coneyislandhistory.org; and honor community leaders and amusement pioneers through the Coney Island Hall of Fame. Emphasizing community involvement, the History Project teaches young people about local history and develops programs in conjunction with local schools, museums, senior centers, and other organizations. (Photograph by Jim McDonell.)

Consistent with our mission to preserve history on a local level, this book was printed in South Carolina on American-made paper and manufactured entirely in the United States. Products carrying the accredited Forest Stewardship Council (FSC) label are printed on 100 percent FSC-certified paper.